Steph King
and
Richard Cooper

MATHS CHALLENGES

MISSION FILE 1
For more able mathematicians in Year 2

Rising Stars UK Ltd, 7 Hatchers Mews, Bermondsey Street, London, SE1 3GS

www.risingstars-uk.com

Published in association with  National Association for Able Children in Education

Published 2014
Text, design and layout © Rising Stars UK Ltd. 2014

Authors: Steph King and Richard Cooper
Series Consultant: Cherri Moseley
Text design and typesetting: Steve Evans Design and Illustration
Cover design: Lon Chan, Words & Pictures Ltd, London
Publisher: Fiona Lazenby
Editorial: Lynette Woodward and Sparks Publishing Services, Ltd
Illustrations: Bill Greenhead (characters) and Steve Evans Design and Illustration

British Library Cataloguing in Publication Data.
A CIP record for this book is available from the British Library.

ISBN: 978-1-78339-229-2

Printed by Newnorth Print, Ltd. Bedford.

Pages 44–45, TASC: Thinking Actively in a Social Context © Belle Wallace 2004

Contents

Welcome to Brain Academy

Da Vinci

The master and founder of Brain Academy. Da Vinci has recently upgraded himself to 'tablet' form. He communicates via his touch screen but doesn't like being prodded and poked by Huxley. Da Vinci is dedicated to eradicating boring maths lessons and solving exciting mathematical problems around the world.

Huxley

Hux is DV's right-hand man. If he can't fix it, no-one can. Huxley carries a 'man-bag' which DV conveniently fits into. Always one for a joke or three, Huxley is the chap who keeps things moving in the right direction. Hopefully, forwards of course.

Rosa

Rosa Spudds is the Brain Academy gardening guru. There is nothing about gardening or 'growing your own' that Rosa doesn't know about. An expert in all fields. (And meadows, hedges, ponds, marshes and farms in general).

Hailey

Hailey Komet gained a PhD in Astrophysics at Oxford. She knows more about wormholes, black holes and any other holes one finds in the depths of the Universe than anyone else on our Planet. Hailey is convinced time travel is possible after the disappearance of the previous team ...

Evan

Evan Elpus is a young inventor from the Welsh Valleys. Da Vinci saw his potential after watching his on-line inventing tutorials, 'Elpus 'Elps You'. Followed everywhere by his Welsh Terrier Dylan, Evan is always up for a challenge. 'Tidy!' as he might say.

Omar

Omar Gosh is the world quiz champion after winning a global edition of 'Faster-mind'. He scored 100% and won on the last question. He knew how tall Mount Everest is ... in centimetres (884,800 cm). As a result, Omar's bank of useful (and useless) knowledge knows no heights.

Gammon

Gammon is the grandson of Ham, the Astro-chimp who flew into space back in 1961. Ham was trained by NASA to pilot a rocket. Gammon has inherited his grandfather's intelligence and has also developed the power of speech. However, this can sometimes be a little awkward due to his, let's say, 'choice of words'. He lives with Hailey Komet whom he 'adopted' earlier.

Mason

Mason Stones is a brilliant architect and master of materials, design and space. He can make any building, anywhere. His constructions are built to survive the elements so hurricanes, tsunamis, volcanoes and earthquakes hold no fear for their occupants. That's his theory anyway – he's still drawing up the plans.

Babs

Ms Barbara 'Babs' Babbage is a distant cousin to Charles Babbage, the inventor of the first computer. Ms Babbage has her own micro-chip like mind which is faster than the zippiest broadband in her home county of Devon. Babs has an accent thicker than clotted cream and a heart as warm as tea.

Echo

Once the hippest chick around, these days **Echonia Plant** (**Echo** to her BA friends!) works at Brain Academy part-time when she's not standing as a Green Party MEP. She knows all there is to know about how HQ runs, so she organises and manages communications. She still heads out into the field for the occasional mission when a nature-loving eco-warrior is needed though!

WPC Gallop and PC Trott

WPC Gallop and PC Trott are fearless police officers who lend a helping hand to the Brain Academy team when criminals are on the loose. Their investigative skills are unparalleled.
They do more than just plod about, you know!

If you ever met the previous Brain Academy team, don't worry they're all okay – I think. They got lost in the Space-time continuum after one of Victor Blastov's 'Time Machine experiments' went wrong. It's just a matter of time before they get back I suppose …

Working with Brain Academy

This tells you where and when each mission takes place. Read the introduction to find out what the problem is and what help the Brain Academy agents need from you.

Start with the Training Mission (TM). This will get you ready for the Main Mission. You will need to use your maths and reasoning skills and explain your thinking.

You will need to find information to help you solve the problems in tables, charts, graphs, and so on. Remember to look carefully!

MISSION 1.13 Going Quackers!

TIME: To ponder?
PLACE: Duck Down

The ducks of Duck Down need to be moved to a bigger pond ... all 100 of them!

These ducks are presenting an ugly problem.

Hmm. We can solve this Omar. If not, the answer will be on the web!

TM

The team has been informed that there are 100 ducks in total that live in three families at the pond. They must move the ducks in their family groups.

		Number of ducks in family
A		multiple of 10 + 1
B		odd number
C		100 ÷ 5

1) Find some possible numbers of ducks that could be in each family.

2) What do you notice about the ducks in **Family B** each time? Why do you think this?

3) Omar counts **nearly 30** ducks in **Family B**. How many ducks are in **Family A**?

32

6

Now you've met the team, you are ready for your mission briefing!

MM

Moving ducks it is not as easy as they think! They must be carried two at a time (one under each arm) to make sure that the little 'duckies' come to no harm.

1) Rosa moves the first four ducks from Family A. How many metres in total must she walk so that she is back at the old pond to pick up the next ducks?

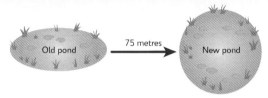
Old pond — 75 metres → New pond

2) Omar moves the first eight ducks from Family B. How many more metres than Rosa has Omar walked so far?

3) Omar has walked 800 metres so far. How do you know that Omar is not yet back at the old pond?

In the Main Mission (MM) you may need to use your answers from the Training Mission to help you. Read the questions carefully and think logically. What information do you have? What do you need to know? Can you use any patterns or rules to help you?

DV FILES

If those pesky pooches harm our ducky friends, I'm sending them the bill!

Oh no! The local doggy walker and five pesky pooches are blocking their way! The two Brain Academy members must split up and go in different directions to avoid the dogs.

Rosa moves her ducks to 33 and then 43 as she notices that the numbers go up in tens, but she is now stuck and must start again!

Find three routes around the grid that follow different number patterns. Write the patterns and explain the rule you used each time to reach the new pond.

93	102	?	?	New pond
?	125	150	51	54
75	50		48	45
66	25	43	39	42
57	Ducks	33	36	44

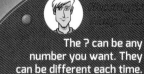

The ? can be any number you want. They can be different each time.

If you're brave enough, try a really tricky challenge from Da Vinci in the DV Files. You'll need to use different problem-solving strategies. It might help to talk to a partner or share ideas in a group.

If you get stuck, call Huxley's Helpline for a hint. There are more Mission Strategies to help you on pages 46 and 47, but have a go yourself first! Remember, Brain Academy agents never give up!

Ready for your first mission? Let's go!

TIME: Time flies!
PLACE: Outside HQ

Unidentified flying objects, UFOs, have been spotted circling the Brain Academy headquarters. Omar thinks they are under attack from aliens! But Huxley notices that the 'UFOs' have strings attached ...

What on earth are they? I've not seen anything like that before!

TM

The unidentified flying objects are getting closer. Omar can just about make out some 2-D shapes.

1) Can you help him name the shapes from the notes he has made?

2) There are two possibilities for the first shape. Write a question you would want to ask to help decide which one it is.

Straight sides	Curved sides	Right angles	Name
4	0	4	
3	0	1	
5	0	0	
1	1	0	
3	0	0	

As the unidentified objects come closer, Omar realises that they are a group of kites fluttering in the wind!

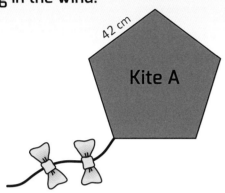

Kite A

42 cm

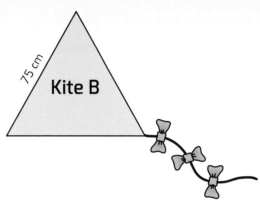

Kite B

75 cm

The frame for each kite is made from pieces of wood. **Kite A** uses five pieces and **Kite B** uses only three.

1) Which kite uses the greatest length of wood in total? How do you know?

2) How many more cm does it use?

DV FILES

Omar decides to play a puzzle game using some of the shapes he has seen and other shapes he knows.

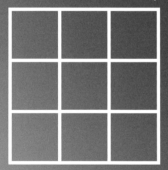

semi-circle
triangle
square
pentagon
rectangle
hexagon
octagon
parallelogram
right-angled triangle

Place all the shapes in the grid so that the shapes in each row have a total of **13** sides **and** the shapes in each diagonal have a total of **11** sides.

Did you hear about the alien who bumped his head?

He saw stars!

Huxley's Helpline

Write the number of sides for each shape first. Remember to include any curved sides.

1.2 Feeling A Bit Drained?

TIME: Desperate O'Clock!
PLACE: Down the drain

A school trip to a Victorian Sewage System has gone wrong ... The lifts are stuck. The shafts are blocked up with – well, goodness knows what.

What have we got in the pipeline, Evan?

A plan to rescue these kids from their stinky situation!

TM

The team look at the records that show how the children had been counted in different group sizes at four locations on the visit.

We still need to find out about the way the group was counted at the information points!

1) Using what you know so far, find all the possible numbers of children on the school trip.

2) The children were counted in groups of fives at Information Point 1. What are the possible numbers of children on the trip now?

Location	Counted in:
Reception	twos
Information Point 1	
Viewing platform	threes
Information point 2	

The team do know that the children all came on one coach that carries a maximum of 55 people.

3) Evan thinks that they do not need to know anything about Information Point 2 now. Do you agree? Explain your thinking.

It is getting rather cold in the lifts and the children have left their coats at Reception! The children read the temperature in the lifts every half hour.

It goes down one section of the scale each time. The thermometer shows one of the temperatures recorded.

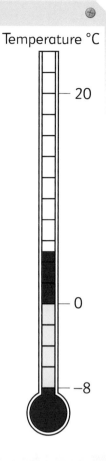

Temperature °C

1) Copy and complete the table to show the temperatures and times.

11 o'clock					Half past 1
		15 °C			

2) At what time did the children read the temperature on the thermometer shown here?

DV FILES

The team must reset the lift control panel to zero before it will work again. Only place value can help them now!

1) The '7' digit can be reset by subtracting two multiples of 10. How many different ways can this be done?

2) Use place value to find all the possible solutions the team used to reset the digits '9' and '6'.

3) Huxley tried to reset the '9' by subtracting 350 and then 550. Explain if you think this idea worked.

Control Panel

9 7 6

The team reset the other digits using two subtractions each time. The lifts start to work and the children are saved, although rather chilly. Phew!

Huxley's Helpline

Here is an example to help you. Seven tens can be reset to zero by subtracting 60 and then 10.

Monkey Mayhem!

TIME: To monkey around
PLACE: Jungle Gym

Hailey and Gammon are turning an old warehouse into a huge indoor playground. Welcome to Monkey Mayhem, where kids can go ape!

There's loads to do-oo-OOO-HHHA-HA for everyone!

TM

Hailey has drawn a plan of the maze.

1) Find the shortest route to go from the green spot ⬤ to the red spot ⬤. Measure it and write the length in centimetres.

2) How many right-angle turns did you need to make?

3) Hailey writes the following statement about the number of clockwise and anti-clockwise turns that will need to be made on the shortest route.

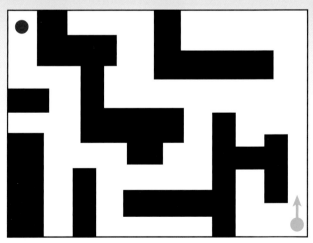

CW turns   >   ACW turns

Find out if the statement is true or correct it if it is false.

The disused warehouse is the perfect place for a super-sized ball pit. The first set of balls is poured into the ball pit.

1) Use the pictures to help you find the fraction of the bag of 24 blue balls and yellow balls used so far.

   Write your answers as _____ of 24 balls = _____ balls

2) Hailey writes these fraction sentences:

   $\frac{1}{4}$ of _____ red balls = 9 balls

   $\frac{1}{3}$ of _____ green balls = 15 balls

How many red balls are there in a full bag? How about green?

DV FILES

The climbing frame will have two ladders, two ropes and a slide.

1) Gammon calculates that the total length of wood needed for the sides of the two ladders is double the total length needed for the steps. Find a way to prove his thinking.

2)

Rope A = multiple of 50 cm

Rope B = double Rope A

Find at least three different possible lengths for Rope A and Rope B.

	Length	Number needed
Ladder sides	2 m for each side	2 for each ladder
Ladder steps	25 cm	8 for each ladder

Huxley's Helpline

What do you know about how many centimetres there are in a metre?

13

TIME: *To catch a giraffe*
PLACE: *Up to your neck in it!*

Gerry the giraffe has escaped from the zoo and is on the run. The team have to track him down and return the escapee to the giraffe house.

Catching this giraffe is going to be a tall order.

We can rise to the challenge, Sir!

TM

Gerry the giraffe eats 44 kg of food and drinks 35 litres of water each day.

	1 day	2 days	3 days	4 days
Food	44 kg			
Water	35 l			

1) Complete the table of giraffe facts.

2) Evan writes 35 x 5 = 175 litres to help him work out how much water the giraffe will drink in 5 days.

Rosa writes 35 ÷ 175 = 5 to check Evan's calculation. What mistake has Rosa made and what should she have done?

The team chase Gerry through the town, but they are finding him very difficult to spot it as he keeps hiding behind objects!

Gerry is 6 m tall.

1) Compare the height of Gerry with the lamp-post. Write the difference in **centimetres**.

2) Now compare Gerry's height with the tree. Write the difference in **metres**.

3) The team spot Gerry trying to hide behind the post box. How much taller is he?

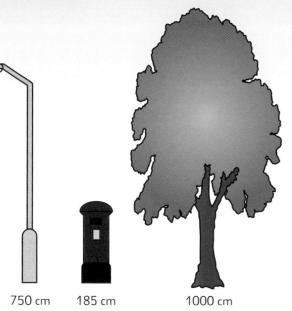

750 cm   185 cm   1000 cm

DV FILES

The team use a rope and some giraffe treats to lead Gerry the giraffe carefully back to the zoo.

1) Investigate to find the shortest route the team can take to return Gerry to the zoo. How many metres is it?

2) The team took a different route. It was 150 m. Find a way to show the route they took. Is there more than one solution?

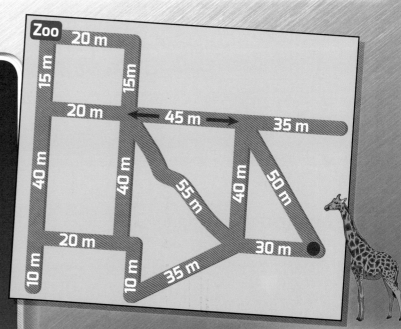

Zoo   20 m
15 m   15 m
20 m   45 m   35 m
40 m   40 m   55 m   40 m   50 m
20 m   30 m
10 m   10 m   35 m

Huxley's Helpline

Try some different routes to begin with to help find the shortest route.

Art Attack!

TIME: The day before opening
PLACE: The Brain Academy Art Gallery

Preparation is under way for the opening of the new Brain Academy Art Gallery.

This exhibition is going to be fabulous, my dear Huxley.

A brush with the art world, Sir. What a picture!

TM

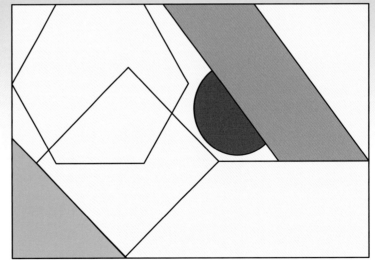

1) Write the names of all the different shapes that you can see.

2) Huxley spots this shape in the picture.

   What is this shape called and how do you know?

3) Find another unusual shape with **straight sides** in the picture. Draw it and explain what you think it might be called. You may need to find out what it is called.

The team get to work mounting all the paintings in wooden frames.

45 cm

75 cm

Flowers

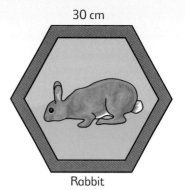

30 cm

Rabbit

1) What length of wood is needed to frame the flower painting?

2) What length of wood is needed to frame the rabbit painting?

3) The team make another 20 hexagonal frames of the same size. How many pieces of 30 cm wood will they need altogether? Write the calculation you used to help you.

DV FILES

Shapes

Flowers

Portrait

Rabbit

The team just cannot decide in what order they should hang the paintings. Investigate to find all the different possibilities that the team can choose. Find a way to organise your solutions.

What a collection! (I'm not telling you which one I painted.)

Huxley's Helpline

Use a code for each painting so you do not need to keep writing it out in full. For example, S for shapes, F for flowers and so on.

TIME: Early morning
PLACE: Beside the seaside

Babs has discovered an old map belonging to her great-great-uncle Arthur. The team investigate, with surprising results.

Can I scan this old map onto your hard drives, DV?

Of course! It is VERY old! Even the lost pier is on it.

TM

The team decide to start by the old pier. They will use what they know about fractions of a whole turn to help them.

1) Using 'F' for forward, direct the team around the old pier and along to see the lifeboats. Remember to say whether the turn is **clockwise or anti-clockwise**.

2) The team walk past the school on their way to the church. Explain why it would be silly for Babs to make an anti-clockwise $\frac{3}{4}$ turn to go to the church.

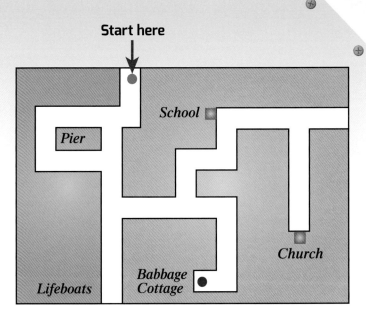

Start here

School

Pier

Church

Babbage Cottage

Lifeboats

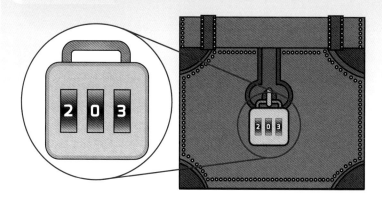

After a while, they stumble across Babbage Cottage. The house is empty, not lived in for years and the door is unlocked! In the corner of the kitchen Babs find a small door to the cellar. Behind it is a treasure chest under a dusty old sheet!

1) Help the team open the chest by using the digits '2', '0' and '3' to make six different numbers. The padlock already shows **2 0 3**. Write each of the numbers you make in words.

2) Now order the numbers from smallest to largest.

3) A sticker on the back of the padlock says **180 less than** the highest combination of 2, 0, 3' . Write the code the team must use.

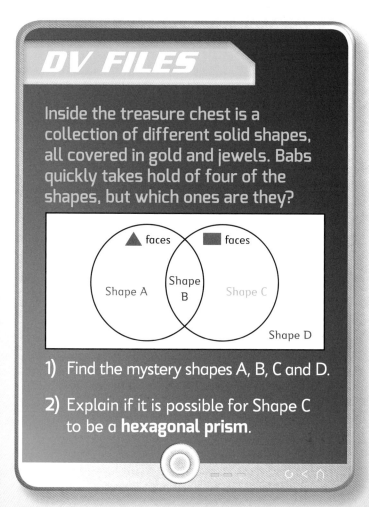

DV FILES

Inside the treasure chest is a collection of different solid shapes, all covered in gold and jewels. Babs quickly takes hold of four of the shapes, but which ones are they?

▲ faces   ■ faces

Shape A   Shape B   Shape C

Shape D

1) Find the mystery shapes A, B, C and D.

2) Explain if it is possible for Shape C to be a **hexagonal prism**.

Our family fortune ... I don't need it: the town can rebuild the old pier with the money. What a nice old lady I am!

Huxley's Helpline

Use a set of 3–D solids to help you. There may be more than one solution!

Star Spotting!

TIME: *After sundown*
PLACE: *Astronomy Club*

It's a normal afternoon for the children in the Astronomy Club – until a new discovery is made.

I think Gammon has discovered a new solar system, DV!

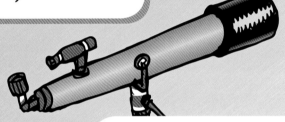

That chimp will make a monkey out of all of us.

TM

The team find out about the number of days each planet in the Solar System takes to orbit the Sun.

1) The digit '6' can be found in five of the numbers. Write its value each time. Neptune is tricky!

2) How many more days does it take the Earth to orbit the Sun than Venus?

3) How can you prove that it takes Mercury **more than 10 weeks** to orbit the Sun?

Planet	Approximate number of days
Mercury	88
Venus	225
Earth	365
Mars	687
Jupiter	4333
Saturn	10,759
Uranus	30,684
Neptune	60,190
Pluto (dwarf planet)	90,465

> Mmm, how strange. I haven't seen those objects before ... the pattern seems to be symmetrical. Maybe the yellow line will help us.

Hailey and the children look through the big telescope.

1) Do you agree with Hailey? Is the pattern symmetrical? Find a way to prove your thinking.

2) Suddenly two more objects, G and H, come into view. They now make the pattern symmetrical. Show the position of G and H on the diagram.

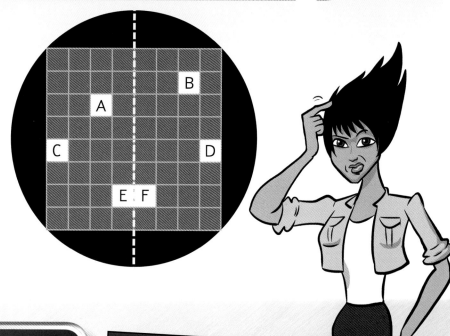

DV FILES

Could it be another Solar System? Are the objects planets? How far away are they from Earth?

The telescope makes everything appear 10 times closer.

1) Help the team complete the missing distances. Write the calculations you use to help you each time.

2) Make up some other distances for Objects E, F, G and H. Put them in a table like this one to show their real distance from Earth and the distance through the telescope.

	Real distance (km)	With telescope (km)
Object A	150	
Object B		230
Object C	950	
Object D		18

> I think my discovery should be named after meHEHEHEHEHE!

Huxley's Helpline

An object that is 40 km away would look like it was only 4 km away!

Rocking Horse Runaways

TIME: *The middle of the night*
PLACE: *Somewhere near you*

Someone has gone round homes at night setting all the rocking horses 'free'. The Brain Academy team have to round them up and return them.

This is outrageous! Rocking horses are very rare these days.

You must be off your rocker to pull a stunt like this.

TM

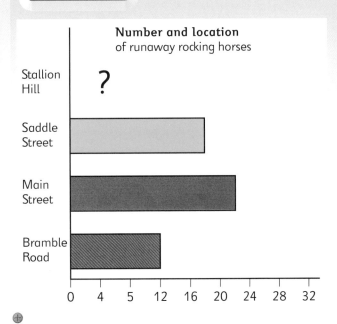

Number and location of runaway rocking horses

Stallion Hill — ?
Saddle Street
Main Street
Bramble Road

0 4 5 12 16 20 24 28 32

The problem is worse than they thought. The bar chart shows the number of runaway horses reported to the police that night.

1) How many more rocking horses escaped from Main Street than Bramble Road?

2) The number from Stallion Hill is half-way between the numbers reported missing from Saddle Street and Main Street. What is it?

3) How many rocking horses are on the run altogether?

The Brain Academy team will need the help of the local police to complete this mission. WPC Gallop and PC Trott join the search on Bramble Street, where the first six horses went missing. Perhaps they can find a clue at one of the houses?

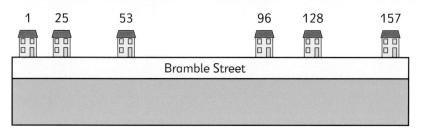

1) How many houses after **house number 1** is **house number 25**?

2) Help the police find each house by telling them how many more houses to count on each time.

3) The seventh rocking horse escaped from the house that is 104 houses after number 157. Which house is this?

Houses on Bramble Street are only on one side of the road.

DV FILES

57	36	27	24	66	24		24	57	36	18	45	69		75	66		63	27	66	66	.
36	63	63		21	36		21	57	66		33	78	27	48	!						

The clues led the police and the BA team to the local park, where the horses were all found to be having a 'rocking' time! Luckily, rocking horses can't move very fast and the team soon have them safely back home. Here is the clue that the police found. **They worked out that the letter Z is 3, Y is 6 and X is 9.**

What was the clue found by the police?

Huxley's Helpline

You may find it easier to write the alphabet first.

TIME: No time to lose
PLACE: At Stonehenge

A plague of moles has been discovered burrowing underneath Stonehenge! The ancient monument is in danger of collapsing into a warren of mole tunnels.

> These moles are tunnelling under Stonehenge. Those stones have stood for thousands of years!

> Not for much longer, unless we stop the moley menaces!

TM

The moles have been very busy digging and moving the soil out of the tunnels.

14 kg only

A team of moles can pull a full load of 14 kg of soil from the tunnels in one trip. When they are feeling tired, they only half-fill the cart.

1) Use this information to help complete this table.

	Number of full loads	Number of half loads	kg of soil moved
First tunnel	3	0	
Second tunnel	5	1	
Third tunnel	5	2	
Fourth tunnel			56

2) The moles can move the 56 kg of soil on their fourth tunnel in different ways. Find another solution.

CHALLENGE: Can you find all solutions?

The team arrive at Stonehenge late at night and catch the moles at work. They see what appear to be four different teams of moles lined up in rows, but they can only see the tops of their hard-hats.

TEAM A

TEAM B

TEAM C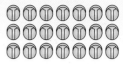

1) Find the total number of moles in each of the teams A, B and C.

2) Write a multiplication (x) to describe each team.

3) Mason counts 36 moles in another team, Team D. How are they arranged? Try to find more than one solution.

4) How many moles did Mason see in total?

DV FILES

The Brain Academy gang must divide and conquer the mole teams. The tunnels must be quickly filled and the entrances sealed while the moles are moved safely away.

	Total number of moles	Fraction of moles that followed Mason	Fraction of moles that followed Evan	Number of moles that followed Hux
Team A		$\frac{1}{4}$	$\frac{1}{3}$	
Team B		$\frac{1}{4}$	$\frac{3}{4}$	
Team C		$\frac{1}{3}$	$\frac{1}{3}$	
Team D	36	$\frac{1}{2}$	$\frac{1}{3}$	

Evan has invented three different 'mole whistles to lure the moles away from Stonehenge, but not all the moles like the same tune the mole-whistles play.

Find out the number of moles from each army that followed Huxley. Show how you worked it out.

Stonehenge is saved for the nation. I think we should put ALL the stones back upright though!

Huxley's Helpline

What do you know about finding fractions of a set of objects?

TIME: To invent something new
PLACE: Rosa's garden

Rosa's new Sweetie Beans will change how kids see vegetables!

> Getting the kids to eat their greens has always 'bean' difficult Rosa, any ideas?

> Try these Sweetie Beans! All the goodness of veggies, but they taste and look like sweets.

Rosa has been working hard on her new invention. The Sweetie Beans must be given the same amount of water every day at the three times shown below.

Morning

Lunch time

Afternon

1) Write the three times in words.

2) Compare the morning and afternoon time. How much later is the afternoon time?

3) The container shows how much water (in millilitres **ml**) is used in the morning. How many **millimetres** of water are used in total each day?

After a week of love and care, the *Sweetie Beans* begin to grow – very quickly! Here is the height of one of the plants on Day 9.

Day 8	Day 9	Day 10	Day 11	Day 12

1) On Day 8, the plant was $3\frac{1}{2}$ cm shorter than on Day 9. Draw and label the height of the plant on **Day 8**. Complete the table for Days 8 and 9.

2) The plant grows $3\frac{1}{2}$ cm every day. Complete the table for Days 10, 11 and 12.

3) On what day will the plant reach $26\frac{1}{2}$ cm tall?

DV FILES

The team pick the Sweetie Beans and put them in bags of 150 beans. Each bag costs £1.25. The local shops order different amounts of beans. Use the information to find out how much they each spend.

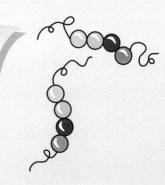

Sweetie Bean order

Super Shopper	10 bags
Great Grocers	600 beans
Windy Corner Shop	7 bags
Pukka Prices	12 bags
Tom's Tasty Treats	900 beans

Huxley's Helpline

How many lots of 25p are in £1?

27

1.11 The Mind Boggles!

TIME: *Holiday time!*
PLACE: *Snorkelling in the sea caves*

Hailey and Huxley investigate sightings of Boggle Fish in the sea caves of Devon.

What do you call a fish with no eyes?

A 'fsh' of course Hux, why do you ask?

TM

1) Describe the fraction of a full turn that Hailey needs to make so she faces the same direction as Huxley. How many right-angle turns is this?

2) They slowly swim to an underwater cave. It takes Huxley 13 minutes to swim there. It takes Hailey 120 seconds more. How long did it take Hailey to swim to the cave?

3) If they started swimming at twenty past eleven, what time did Hailey reach the cave?

As Huxley and Hailey reach the mouth of the cave, they are greeted by lots of 'boggly' eyes staring at them!

1) How many *two-eyed Boggle Fish* have the same number of eyes as 4 *three-eyed Boggle Fish*?

2) How many *three-eyed Boggle Fish* will have the same number of eyes as 15 *two-eyed Boggle Fish*?

3) Make up some examples of your own.
   e.g. _____ *three-eyed Boggle Fish* will have the same number of eyes as _____ *two-eyed Boggle Fish*.

DV FILES

Huxley took two photos of the different Boggle Fish, but it was difficult to see how many of each are in the pictures. Only eyes could be seen ...

1) Find some different possible numbers of *two-eyed* and *three-eyed* Boggle Fish in each photograph. There is more than one solution each time.

2) Describe any patterns you notice.

Photograph 1

30 eyes in total

Photograph 2

39 eyes in total

Huxley's Helpline

Think about using a table to help you organise your ideas.

1.12 Ham the Astro-Chimp

TIME: *Late evening*
PLACE: *Under the microscope*

Gammon's grandpa was called Ham. He was a real-life spacecraft flying chimpanzee!

Are those microbes? I think they are-AH-AH-AH!

We've been studying Ham's old spacesuit for hours. Look at all that old space-dust. Can you see through the microscope?

TM

The strange bacteria appear as different shapes under the microscope.

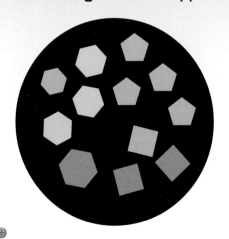

1) What fraction of the total shapes are pentagons?

2) What fraction of the total shapes are squares?

3) What is the name of the other shape?

4) On a different part of Ham's space suit, they find bacteria that appear as a mystery shape with eight vertices (or corners). Draw and name the mystery shape.

The bacteria are all over Ham's space suit! The table shows the number of samples of each bacteria found on different parts of the suit.

Complete the information in the table for each shape.

	Head	Arm	Leg	Back	Front
⬠	23			83	
◼			77		
⬡	29				

1) The number of ⬠ samples increases by 20 each time.

2) The samples for the square increase by 30 each time.

3) The number of samples of ⬡ increases by 40 each time.

DV FILES

Hailey and Gammon also found many samples of a mystery shape with eight vertices (corners). Use the clues to find how many samples were found on each part of Ham's space suit.

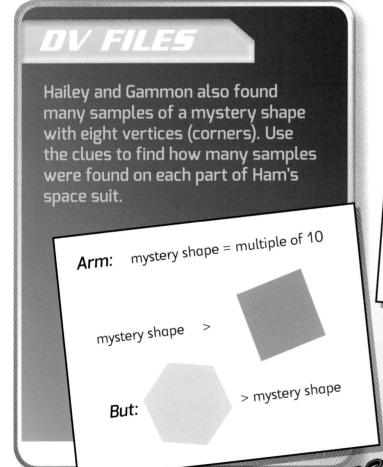

Arm: mystery shape = multiple of 10

mystery shape   >

But: > mystery shape

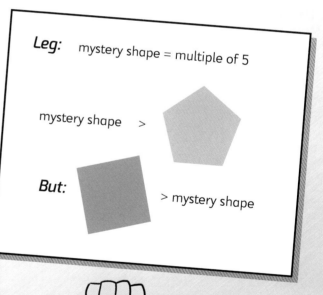

Leg: mystery shape = multiple of 5

mystery shape   >

But: > mystery shape

Try to find the largest and smallest possible number of samples each time.

TIME: To ponder?
PLACE: Duck Down

The ducks of Duck Down need to be moved to a bigger pond ... all 100 of them!

These ducks are presenting an ugly problem.

Hmm. We can solve this Omar. If not, the answer will be on the web!

TM

The team has been informed that there are 100 ducks in total that live in three families at the pond. They must move the ducks in their family groups.

	Number of ducks in family
A	 multiple of 10 + 1
B	odd number
C	100 ÷ 5

1) Find some possible numbers of ducks that could be in each family.

2) What do you notice about the ducks in **Family B** each time? Why do you think this?

3) Omar counts **nearly 30** ducks in **Family B**. How many ducks are in **Family A**?

Moving ducks it is not as easy as they think! They must be carried two at a time (one under each arm) to make sure that the little 'duckies' come to no harm.

1) Rosa moves the first four ducks from Family A. How many metres in total must she walk so that she is back at the old pond to pick up the next ducks?

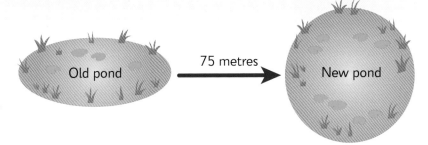

2) Omar moves the first eight ducks from Family B. How many more metres than Rosa has Omar walked so far?

3) Omar carries on until he has walked 800 metres in total. How do you know that he is not yet back at the old pond?

DV FILES

Oh no! The local doggy walker and five pesky pooches are blocking their way! The two Brain Academy members must split up and go in different directions to avoid the dogs.

Rosa moves her ducks to 33 and then 43 as she notices that the numbers go up in tens, but she is now stuck and must start again!

Find three routes around the grid that follow different number patterns. Write the patterns and explain the rule you used each time to reach the new pond.

If those pesky pooches harm our ducky friends, I'm sending them the bill!

93	102	?	?	New pond
?	125	150	51	54
75	50		48	45
66	25	43	39	42
57	Ducks	33	36	44

Huxley's Helpline

The ? can be any number you want. They can be different each time.

TIME: To go shopping
PLACE: On the Internet

The Brain Academy team are buying birthday presents for Da Vinci. However, it's hard to know what to buy a tablet! What should they get him?

Well, personal hygiene is important, even for old tablets who reset their age on their hard drives. Da Vinci says he's only 4 GB old!

I think we should buy both items from Tablet Things as the case is much cheaper!

TM

The team begin with a search for a new charger and case.

	Charger	Case
Tablet Things	£7	£15
PC Prices	£6.75	£15.25

1) Do you agree with Babs? Explain your thinking.

2) How much change will they get from £30 if they buy both items at *PC Prices?*

3) What should they do so they pay the least amount for both items?

4) How much change from £30 will they have now?

The team are looking at the cost of screen wipes on different Internet sites. They would like to buy 30 wipes for Da Vinci.

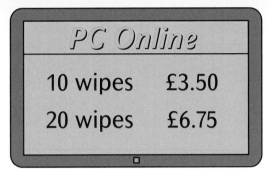

PC Online

| 10 wipes | £3.50 |
| 20 wipes | £6.75 |

ON THE WEB

| 5 wipes | £1.70 |
| 10 wipes | £3.95 |

1) Find the best price for buying 30 wipes at *PC Online*. Show the two different ways in which 30 wipes can be bought.

2) Now find all the different ways that 30 wipes can be bought from *On the Web*.

3) What should the team do to get the best value for money?

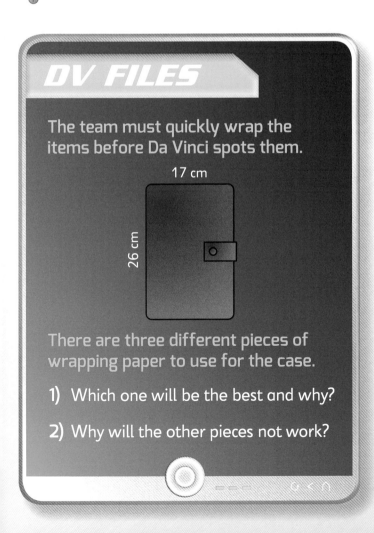

DV FILES

The team must quickly wrap the items before Da Vinci spots them.

17 cm

26 cm

There are three different pieces of wrapping paper to use for the case.

1) Which one will be the best and why?

2) Why will the other pieces not work?

32 cm

30 cm

Paper A

25 cm

45 cm

Paper B

28 cm

37 cm

Paper C

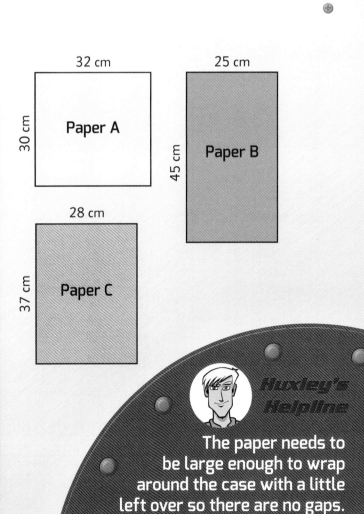

Huxley's Helpline

The paper needs to be large enough to wrap around the case with a little left over so there are no gaps.

TIME: *To get organised*
PLACE: *Brain Academy HQ*

Huxley is trying to organise Da Vinci and get his diary in order.

Time to re-charge your batteries, Sir, and dust off your cases.

Sounds like you're taking me on holiday, old boy!

Monday	Friday
Morning	
9 o'clock — Team meeting	
half past 11 — Battery charge	
Tuesday	**Saturday**
Morning	
1/4 past 10 — Team meeting	
12 o'clock — Check e-mails	
Wednesday	**Sunday**
Morning	
quarter to 10 — Team meeting	
1 o'clock — Video call	
Thursday	**Notes**
	Check BA news daily
	Write meeting notes

1) Help Huxley to write in the Team meetings for the rest of the week. All meetings are after *half past 8*, but before *half past 10*. No meetings start at the same time.

2) Da Vinci always needs to charge his battery $2\frac{1}{2}$ hours after the start of the team meeting. What time will this be on Tuesday and Wednesday?

3) The battery must charge for 1 hour before a **video call** can be made. Do you think Huxley has left enough time? Explain your thinking.

MM

Huxley always sings his own version of the song to help him remember the number of days in each month. Brain Academy have team meetings **every** day of the year.

Thirty days has September,
April, June and November,
All the rest have thirty-one,
except for February alone,
which has twenty-eight days rain or shine,
but in a leap year, twenty-nine.

Months grouped in threes			Total
January	February	March	91
April	May	June	
July	August	September	
October	November	December	

1) Find the total number of meetings that take place in different parts of the year.

2) Explain what the total of 91 tells you about January, February and March in this year.

DV FILES

Da Vinci makes a video call every Wednesday.

Huxley wants to book 9 video calls altogether for March and April. Here is the start of the calendar for March.

Find a way to prove to Huxley that this is not possible.

March

M	TU	W	TH	F	SA	SU
			1	2	3	4
5	6	7	8	9	10	11

Sir, why did the chicken cross the Internet?

To get to the other site, of course!

Huxley's Helpline

What do you know about the number of days in March and April?

TIME: To help out
PLACE: At the police station and fire station

The Brain Academy team are helping make sure all the police and fire equipment meets the health and safety rules!

> Oh dear! Lots of the police and fire equipment is broken.

> Don't worry: we can fix the old stuff with some brain power!

TM

WPC Gallop shows the team to the room where all the broken equipment is stored.

1) The small ladder should have six steps in total. Two steps are broken. What fraction of the total steps is broken?

2) The same fraction is broken on the medium and on the tall ladder. Four steps are broken on the medium ladder and six are broken on the tall ladder. How many steps **should** be on each ladder in total?

In a large box there are lots of pieces of hosepipe.
Each piece is $\frac{1}{4}$ or $\frac{1}{2}$ of the whole hosepipe.

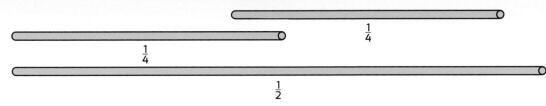

1) Complete the table to show different ways to make whole hosepipes.

$\frac{1}{2}$ of whole pipe pieces	$\frac{1}{4}$ of whole pipe pieces	Whole hose pipes
2	0	1
0		1
		2
		2
		3

2) Evan puts together six lots of ¼ pipes and four lots of ½ pipes to make a long hosepipe. How long is the long hosepipe now? Prove your answer by drawing a number line.

DV FILES

There are four boxes of truncheons: all 56 of them need their handles mending. There is the same number of truncheons in each box.

1) How many truncheons are in each box?

It is thirsty work and four team members stop for some water. They each drink an equal amount but 250 ml is still left in the jug.

2) How much water did each team member drink?

- 1 litre
- 900
- 800
- 700
- 600
- 500
- 400
- 300
- 200
- 100

Huxley's Helpline

Think about the calculations you can write out to help you.

TIME: To get building
PLACE: In Newtown

Mason has been called in to design new homes.

New homes for people are needed, Mason. Can you help?

Of course, I have already drawn up some plans, Sir.

TM

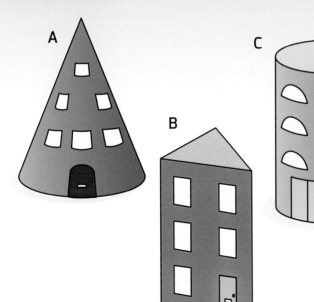

A

B

C

1) What is the shape of each of Mason's new buildings?

2) How many rectangular faces will Mason need for six shape B buildings?

3) There is the same number of windows on each face of building B. How many windows will be needed for the six buildings?

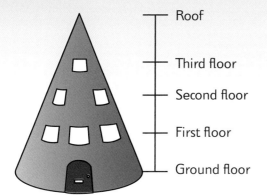

Roof

Third floor

Second floor

First floor

Ground floor

Mason has designed a spiral staircase for the centre of building A. Building A has four floors altogether, but no steps are needed to get to the ground floor. Mason has planned for 96 steps in total. An equal number of steps are used between each floor.

1) How many steps will Mason have to climb to reach the second floor?

2) How many steps will Mason have to take in total to go from the ground floor to the first floor and then back again?

3) He uses 23 m 50 cm of handrail for each set of stairs. How much will he use in total?

DV FILES

Mason is very proud of his designs, but he has forgotten something very important! Each room in bulding A needs a main door!

Use the clues to work out how much Mason must spend on doors.

- The ground floor has 20 more main doors than the third floor.
- Doors cost £100 each.
- There are 12 main doors on the second floor.
- The third floor has $\frac{3}{4}$ of the number of main doors as the second floor.
- The first floor has double the number of main doors as the third floor.

Did you hear about the magic dumper truck?

Yes, it turned into a building site!

Huxley's Helpline

Find out how many doors there are on each floor first.

TIME: Before school
PLACE: Sausage City

The children of Sausage City are not getting their '5-a-day' fruit and vegetables. Huxley and Rosa know that a balanced diet is essential!

Wow, they eat 30 more Sizzle Sausages than Spicy Sausages! That's a lot of sausage ...

These children need feeding properly. It's a fruitless task, Huxley.

TM

The pictogram shows the different varieties of sausage and how many are eaten each week by an average primary school class in Sausage City.

Use all the information to find out the following:

1) How many sausages does each 'whole' sausage 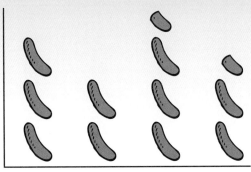 in the pictogram show?

2) How can you prove that the children eat exactly 75 of one variety of sausage?

3) What is the **total** number of Super and Saucy sausages eaten by the class in a week?

| Super Sausage | Saucy Sausage | Sizzle Sausage | Spicy Sausage |

 = _____ sausages

The Brain Academy team must get to work. They record the number of bags of each fruit they plan to deliver to each school. Fruit is packed in bags of **2 kg**.

1) Use the information to copy and complete the tally chart.

2) What is the total mass of fruit to be delivered to each school?

3) The team will deliver fruit to **five** schools in Sausage City. How many **more** bags of bananas than apples will be delivered in total? Explain your decision.

	Bags of fruit	Total in kg
Apples	|||| |||| ||||	
Bananas	|||| |||| |||| |||	
Pears		24 kg

DV FILES

It takes the team **15 minutes** to reach Sausage School and make the delivery. It takes them **30 minutes** to drive the **15 km** to deliver fruit to Bangers School. **They drive at the same speed for all deliveries.**

1) Use all the information to show if the team make it to all the schools in time for them to have their fruit delivery before morning playtime.

2) What time did they arrive at Mash School?

3) The journey from Gravy School back to base is **10 km**. What time did they arrive back at base?

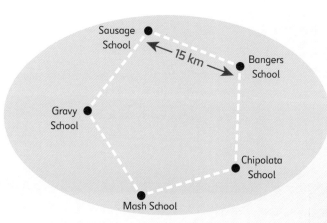

It is 8 o'clock in the morning. Will the team get the fruit from the base to all schools by morning playtime at half past 10?

What do you know about the properties of a regular pentagon?

Problem-solving Strategies

Use the TASC Problem Solving Wheel to help you. TASC means Thinking Actively in a Social Context.

Reflect
What have I learned?

Communicate
Who can I tell?

Evaluate
Did I succeed? Can I think of another way?

Implement
Now let me do it!

Learn from experience

Communicate

What have I learned?

Let's tell someone.

How well did I do?

Evaluate

Let's do it!

TA

Implement

We can learn to be expert thinkers!

Gather/organise

What do I know about this?

Identify

What is the task?

Generate

How many ideas can I think of?

Decide

Which is the best idea?

Gather/organise

What do I know about this?

Identify

What is the task?

Generate

How many ideas can I think of?

Decide

Which is the best idea?

T S C

Mission Strategies

Mission 1.1

For the Training Mission, you may find it helpful to use a set of solid shapes to check your thinking.

Mission 1.2

You will need to use the picture in the Main Mission to first work out the scale on the thermometer.

Mission 1.3

In the Main Mission, you will need to use your multiplication and division facts to help you work with these fractions.

Mission 1.4

Think about how you can use doubling to complete the table in the Training Mission.

Mission 1.5

Use what you know about 2-D shapes to help find any missing lengths on the two picture frames. This will help you in the Main Mission.

Mission 1.6

Remember that clockwise describes a turn that moves in the same direction as the hands on a clock. So anti-clockwise is a turn in the opposite direction.

Mission 1.7

A mirror will help you look for symmetrical patterns in the Main Mission.

Mission 1.8

Look for any patterns in the numbers that stand for letters X, Y and Z in the Da Vinci Files. What do you think comes next?

Mission 1.9

Knowing half of 14 will help you in the Training Mission!

Mission 1.10

How many centimetres does the plant grow every two days? The answer to this question will help you in the Main Mission.

Mission 1.11

For these missions, you may want to make a list of the total number of eyes each time as you count the different Boggle-fish. Look for any numbers that are in both lists.

Mission 1.12

You will need to use your completed table from the Main Mission to help you in the Da Vinci Files. Remember to check to see if the sign used for each number sentence is < , > or =.

Mission 1.13

Remember that 75m is the distance from the old pond to the new pond. What do you know about the journey back to the old pond? Rosa and Omar must return to the old pond each time in the Main Mission.

Mission 1.14

In the Da Vinci Files, remember that you can turn the case around to check to see if there is enough wrapping paper.

Mission 1.15

You can use a clock resource to help you work out the times in the Training Mission.

Mission 1.16

How many quarters are equal to one half? The answer to this question will help you in the Main Mission!

Mission 1.17

For the Main Mission, you will need to think about the number of sets of steps there are in Mason's spiral staircase. Remember that no steps are needed to get up to the ground floor.

Mission 1.18

When you are solving the Da Vinci File problem, don't forget to include the 15 minutes that it takes to drive from the Brain Academy base to Sausage School.

National Association for Able Children in Education

What is NACE?

NACE, a registered charity founded in 1983, is the leading independent organisation for the education of the more able.

What does NACE do?

NACE specialises in working with teachers and schools to improve learning for the more able and to turn ability into achievement for all.

The NACE community provides teachers with:
A members' website including:
- Guidance and resources
- New to A,G&T
- Subject specific resources
- Specialist advice
- An award winning monthly E-bulletin packed with sources of inspiration and regular updates
- NACE Insight, a termly newsletter

How will the book help me?

The *Brain Academy* Maths Mission Files challenge and help you to become better at learning and a better mathematician by:
- thinking of and testing different solutions to problems
- making connections to what you already know
- working by yourself and with others
- expecting you to get better and to go on to the next book
- learning skills which you can use in other subjects and out of school.

We hope you enjoy the books!